* * * * * * * * * * * *

WAR TRICKS

* * * * * * * * * * * *

→→ By Virginia Loh-Hagan ←←

 **45th Parallel Press**

Published in the United States of America by Cherry Lake Publishing Group
Ann Arbor, Michigan
www.cherrylakepublishing.com

Reading Adviser: Beth Walker Gambro, MS, Ed., Reading Consultant, Yorkville, IL
Book Designer: Melinda Millward

Photo Credits: cover, title page: © Peyker/Shutterstock; page 7: Rama, CC BY-SA 3.0 FR, via Wikimedia Commons; page 9: Beibaoke1/Dreamstime.com; page 11: © FXQuadro/Shutterstock; page 12: Fotokon/Dreamstime.com; page 15: Gary Todd from Xinzheng, China, CC0, via Wikimedia Commons; page 17: J. F. Horrabin (Illustrator), Public domain, via Wikimedia Commons; page 19: WMrapids, CC BY-SA 4.0, via Wikimedia Commons; page 21: Smithsonian American Art Museum, The Ray Austrian Collection, Gift of Beatrice L. Austrian, Caryl A. Austrian and James A. Austrian; page 23: National Portrait Gallery, Smithsonian Institution; Frederick Hill Meserve Collection; page 25: NSA, Public domain, via Wikimedia Commons; page 27: © Carlos Jose Corts/Shutterstock; page 28: © View Apart/Shutterstock

Graphic Element Credits: Cover, multiple interior pages: © marekuliasz/Shutterstock, © Andrey_Kuzmin/Shutterstock, © Here/Shutterstock

Library of Congress Cataloging-in-Publication Data has been filed and is available at catalog.loc.gov.

Cherry Lake Publishing Group would like to acknowledge the work of the Partnership for 21st Century Learning, a Network of Battelle for Kids. Please visit http://www.battelleforkids.org/networks/p21 for more information.

Printed in the United States of America
Corporate Graphics

About the Author

Dr. Virginia Loh-Hagan is an author and educator. She is currently the Director of the Asian Pacific Islander Desi American (APIDA) Center at San Diego State University and the Co-Executive Director of The Asian American Education Project. She lives in San Diego with her very tall husband and very naughty dogs.

Note from publisher: Websites change regularly, and their future contents are outside of our control.
Supervise children when conducting any recommended online searches for extended learning opportunities.

TABLE OF CONTENTS

Introduction 4

Case 1: Persian Cat War (525 BCE) 6

Case 2: Mind Games at Yongqiu (756) 8

Case 3: Fake Death of Viking King (c. 1015–1066) 10

Case 4: Ambushed by Genghis Khan (1162–1227) 14

Case 5: Ottomans' Sailing on Land (1453) 16

Case 6: Lacrosse for the Win (1763) 18

Case 7: Elizabeth Van Lew's Secret Codes (1818–1900).... 20

Case 8: Marching in Yorktown (1862) 22

Case 9: Great Seal Bug (1945) 24

Case 10: Vietcong Military Tactics (1940s–1970s) 26

For Your Eyes Only 30

Glossary 32

Learn More! 32

Index 32

* * * * * * * * * * * *
INTRODUCTION
* * * * * * * * * * *

There is an old saying: *All's fair in love and war*. What do you think this means? Do you agree?

War is **armed** conflict. Armed means having weapons. Nations fight for different reasons. They may want freedom. They may want lands. They may want resources. Some nations attack. Some defend.

The causes differ. But the effects are the same. Many people die. Many get hurt. Cities are destroyed. War affects everyone.

Nations want to be **victors**. Victors are winners. Nations need soldiers. They need weapons. They need **tactics**. Tactics are plans. Some are easy. Some are hard. Some are clever. Learn about famous war tricks in history.

CURRENT CASE:

Drones Drone On and On

* * * * * * * * * *

Future warfare may not need humans. Machines may be the future fighters. Victors will be nations with the best technology. Unmanned military technology means machines run by computers. It doesn't need human pilots. An example is combat drones. Drones are small planes. They get into small spaces. They cover large areas. They safely get into war zones. They get information. They spy. They take pictures. They attack. They drop bombs. Humans control them from afar.

Drones were first used as a deadly weapon in 2001. Today, drone strikes are more common. But drones are more than weapons. They deliver food. They deliver medicine. They deliver supplies. Drones are tools. Tools can be used for peace. Or they can be used for war. Humans aren't needed to run drones. But they still control how they're used.

PERSIAN CAT WAR
(525 BCE)

Ancient Egyptians loved cats. Cats were **sacred**. Sacred means holy. Cats were treated like gods. Egyptians protected cats. They wouldn't hurt them. Persians knew this. They used it against them.

Egypt and Persia were at war. The Battle of Pelusium was the first fight. Pelusium was an Egyptian city. Persian troops invaded the city. They carried cats into battle. The cats were placed in front of them.

Egyptians were surprised. They didn't fight back. They
didn't shoot arrows. They didn't want to harm the cats.
They lost. More than 50,000 Egyptians died. About
7,000 Persians died. Persians took over. They ruled
Egypt for 200 years.

Bastet was an Egyptian goddess. She was a cat goddess.

* * * * * * * * * * * *
MIND GAMES AT YONGQIU
(756)
* * * * * * * * * * * *

Yongqiu is in China. Zhang Xun (709–757) was inside the castle. His army had 2,000 men. The enemy army was outside the castle. They had 40,000 men.

Zhang's troops played war drums. They acted like they were getting ready to fight. They did this for many nights. They kept their enemies awake. This made them tired. The enemy let down their guard. They ignored the drums. Zhang attacked.

Zhang's troops ran out of arrows. Zhang had **scarecrows** made. Scarecrows are straw figures. Zhang dressed them like soldiers. He sent them to the enemy. The enemy opened fire. Zhang took back the scarecrows. He used the arrows. He sent human troops. The enemy thought they were scarecrows. Zhang attacked. He won.

A statue of Zhang Xun stands in *Shuang Miao*, or the Double Temple.

FAKE DEATH OF VIKING KING
(c. 1015–1066)

Harald Sigurdsson (c. 1015–1066) was the king of Norway. He was the last great **Viking** king. Vikings were Norsemen. They were pirates. They were known for raiding. **Sagas** were written about Sigurdsson. Sagas are stories about heroes.

Sigurdsson led armies. Rulers hired him to fight. Sigurdsson invaded Sicily. This happened around 1040. Sicily is an island. It's part of Italy.

Harald Sigurdsson is called "Harald the Ruthless."

Harald Sigurdsson waited outside Sicily's city walls. People thought he was dead. He used this to his advantage.

Sigurdsson camped. He was outside Sicily's city walls. He got sick. He stayed in bed. No one saw him. People thought he was dead. His troops begged Sicily's leaders to let them in. They said Sigurdsson wanted to be buried in a church. The Sicilians let them in. Sigurdsson and his troops attacked. They looted the city.

COLD CASE:

The Unsolved Mystery of Die Glocke

The Nazi Party ruled Germany. They ruled from 1933 to 1945. Their leader was Adolf Hitler (1889–1945). The Nazis fought in World War II. They lost. But they built high-tech weapons. They had better tanks. They had better fighter jets. They had better missiles. Some people think Nazi scientists made a secret "wonder weapon." They called it "Die Glocke." Die Glocke means "the bell." The weapon was shaped like a bell. It glowed. It rotated. It was 12 feet (3.7 meters) high. It was 9 feet (2.7 m) wide. It was a UFO. UFO means unidentified flying object. It served as a time machine. The Nazis lost the war. They wanted to go back in time. They wanted to change history. Die Glocke was in a secret location. It was built underground. No one knows where it is. There are many ideas about it. But there's no proof of Die Glocke. Many think it's a hoax. A hoax is a trick.

AMBUSHED BY GENGHIS KHAN (1162–1227)

Genghis Khan (1162–1227) ruled the Mongol Empire. Mongolia is between Russia and China. Khan's army had more than 80,000 fighters. They killed about 40 million people. They destroyed many cities.

Khan studied his enemies. He messed with them. He pretended to quit. Then he'd attack. He planned surprise attacks. He took hostages. He used people as shields. He asked people to **surrender** or die. Surrender means to give up.

Khan used a spy network. He called this the "yam." The yam was a system of huts. Huts were like stations. They were all over. Riders went from hut to hut. They carried messages. They changed horses at each hut. They covered about 200 miles (322 kilometers) a day.

Genghis Khan is known as one of history's greatest conquerors.

OTTOMANS SAILING ON LAND (1453)

* * * * * * * * * * * *

The Ottoman Empire ruled the Middle East area. In 1453, they invaded Constantinople. Constantinople was the Roman Empire's capital. It's in Turkey. It became the Ottoman Empire's capital. Today, it's called Istanbul.

Constantinople was protected. The Golden Horn was a body of water. It connected the city to the sea. Chains blocked its entrance. Enemy ships couldn't pass.

The Ottomans lifted their ships out of the water. They did this at night. They used log rollers. They rolled their ships over land. They did this for 2 to 3 miles (3.2 to 4.8 km). They got past the chains. They moved their ships back into the water. They blocked supplies. They attacked. The city fell.

The Ottoman Empire was founded in Turkey.

* * * * * * * * * * * *
LACROSSE FOR THE WIN
(1763)
* * * * * * * * * * * *

The Ojibwe live around the Great Lakes. They have a game called baggataway. It's like lacrosse. Lacrosse is an Indigenous sport, too.

Fort Michilimackinac was in Michigan. It had soldiers. It had French settlers. It had English settlers. The Ojibwe camped next to the fort. In 1763, they held a baggataway game. The game was a trick. The Ojibwe invited soldiers to watch. The soldiers left their weapons. They left the fort gates open.

The ball went over the wall. Ojibwe players rushed inside the fort. They took weapons. They attacked. They killed soldiers. They took hostages. They held the fort for a year. Then the British regained control.

Fort Michilimackinac is located on the Straits of Mackinac in Michigan.

ELIZABETH VAN LEW'S SECRET CODES (1818–1900)

Elizabeth Van Lew (1818–1900) was a spy. She served during the American Civil War (1861–1865). Northern states fought Southern states.

Van Lew lived in Richmond, Virginia. But she supported the North. She pretended to support the South. She wrote in a secret diary. She buried the diary in her backyard.

Van Lew helped prisoners of war. She gave them food. She gave them medicine. She helped them escape. She had a network of spies. She sent information to the

North. She hid news in books. She hid news in dishes.
She wrote in code. She used a colorless ink. The ink
turned black when milk was added.

**Elizabeth Van Lew helped prisoners of war.
She also had a secret network of spies.**

MARCHING IN YORKTOWN
(1862)

Yorktown is in Virginia. It was a battle site during the Civil War. The Northern army aimed to take Yorktown. It had 121,000 men. John B. Magruder (1807–1871) was a general. He fought for the South. His job was to protect Yorktown. But he had only 12,000 men. His small army didn't stand a chance.

Magruder put on a show. He painted logs black. The logs looked like weapons. His troops played drums. They marched over and over. They used the same men. But they made it look like many different men were marching. Magruder's trick worked. It slowed the Northern army. This bought Magruder time. He got more troops.

Magruder's troops played drums and marched the same men over and over. This made their small army seem larger.

GREAT SEAL BUG

(1945)

W. Averell Harriman (1891–1986) was a U.S. **ambassador**. Ambassadors represent a country. Harriman was living in Moscow. Moscow is Russia's capital.

Russian children visited Harriman's house. They brought a gift. The gift was a wooden sign. It had the Great Seal of the United States. Harriman hung it in his house.

But it had a hidden **bug**. A bug is a listening device. It was one of the first of its kind. Russians **eavesdropped**.

Eavesdrop means to listen without permission. Russians spied on Harriman. They did this for 7 years.

The British found the bug. They studied it. They improved it. They built a better device.

The bug was called "The Thing." It was invented by Leon Theremin (1896–1993).

OPEN DOOR
SLOWLY

VIETCONG MILITARY TACTICS
(1940s–1970s)

The Vietnam War (1954–1975) was in Southeast Asia. North Vietnam fought South Vietnam. The United States sent troops. They supported South Vietnam. The Northern Vietnamese armies had special fighters. They were called the Vietcong. They wanted to spread **communism**. Communist governments own all property and businesses.

The Vietcong built hidden tunnels. They did this for more than 200 miles (322 km). They dug them out by hand. The tunnels had hospitals. They had weapons.

They had sleeping areas. They had kitchens. They had water sources. The Vietcong hid there. They escaped there for safety. They could attack from anywhere. The tunnels also had booby traps. They had spikes. They had small bombs. They had snakes.

The United States entered the Vietnam War in 1965. The U.S. Army was on the side of South Vietnam. It wanted to stop communism.

The Vietcong used hidden tunnels.

U.S. soldiers found the tunnels. They launched an operation. Soldiers would search the tunnels. They called the soldiers tunnel rats. The soldiers were small. They crawled in dark places. They looked for traps. They looked for the enemy. They captured thousands. They found important information.

The United States pulled out of the war. North Vietnam and the Vietcong won.

WORST-CASE SCENARIO:

Atomic Bomb as End Game

* * * * * * * * * * *

The United States made atomic bombs. Atomic bombs are deadly. They use nuclear power. They explode into large fireballs. They spread radiation. Radiation can be deadly. Atomic bombs destroy everything. They were first used during World War II. Their creation was called the Manhattan Project (1942–1945). The United States wanted to end World War II. They dropped atomic bombs on Japan. This happened in 1945. The bombs killed more than 100,000 people. They destroyed 2 cities.

Now, many countries have nuclear weapons. If a country uses one, others will use them in response. A nuclear war would be the end game. The end game means the end of humanity. More than half of the world's people would die. Many more would be hurt or sick. Water would be poisoned. Plants and animals would die.

FOR YOUR EYES ONLY...

* * * * * * * * * *

HOW TO PLAN A WAR TRICK!*

Do you want to plan a war trick? Do you have what it takes? Here are 3 tips:

Tip #1: Know your enemy.

Knowledge is power. Learn everything about the other side. Learn their strengths. Learn their weak spots. Learn who the leaders are. Learn their reasons for fighting.

Tip #2: Know your resources.

Work with what you have. Work with your strengths. Know your fighters. Know their skills. Know your area. Know where you can do sneak attacks.

Tip #3: Know your weak spots.

Enemies will attack weak spots. Protect any weak spots. Build more defenses.

*WARNING: War is not a game. You must be 18 years old to join the U.S. military.

ICYW: IN CASE YOU'RE WONDERING...

The Science Behind War

* * * * * * * * * *

Humans fight. They kill. They do this for personal reasons. They may be protecting their homes. They may be protecting their families. They may seek revenge. But war is different. War is social. Groups organize to kill people from other groups. Some scientists think humans are designed for war. Humans make war to get rid of competitors. They keep out outsiders. They get land. They get resources. There's another idea. Some scientists think humans are like doves. They think humans aren't designed for war. Humans make war because of society. Scientists study the history of war. They look at art. They look at weapons. They look at remains. They think the first war began around 9700 BCE. Humans settled. They began to form complex societies. There were more people in one space. This created reasons for war.

GLOSSARY

ambassador (am-BAH-suh-duhr) a person sent by a country as its official representative to a foreign country

armed (ARMD) equipped with weapons

bug (BUHG) a hidden listening device used to monitor or record someone's conversations

communism (KAHM-yuh-nih-zuhm) a government in which goods and services are owned communally; opposite of democracy and capitalism

eavesdropped (EEVZ-drahpd) secretly listened to a conversation

sacred (SAY-kruhd) holy or blessed

sagas (SAH-guhs) long stories about heroes

scarecrows (SKAHR-krohz) a straw figure made to look like a human

surrender (suh-REHN-duhr) to give up

tactics (TAK-tiks) actions or strategies designed to achieve a goal

victors (VIK-tuhrs) people who defeat an enemy or opponent

Viking (VY-king) a Scandinavian seafaring pirate and trader in the 8th to 11th centuries

LEARN MORE!

Gaertner, Meg. *US Air Force*. Mendota Heights, MN: North Star Editions, 2022.

Loh-Hagan, Virginia. *Weird Science: Military*. Ann Arbor, MI: 45th Parallel Press, 2021.

Meister, Cari. *Totally Amazing Facts about Military Vehicles*. North Mankato, MN: Capstone Press, 2017.

Spears, James, and John Perritano. *Everything Battles: Arm Yourself with Fierce Photos and Fascinating Facts*. Washington, DC: National Geographic Kids, 2013.

INDEX

American Civil War, 20–21, 22–23
army size, 8–9, 14, 22–23
atomic bomb, 29

British soldiers, 18–19
bugs, 24–25

cats, 7–8
codes, 20–21
cold cases, 13
Cold War, 24–25, 29
communication networks, 15, 20–21
Constantinople, 16–17

disarming techniques, 6–7, 9, 18–19
drones, 5
drums, 8, 22–23

Egypt, 7–8

faked deaths, 10–12
Fort Michilimackinac, 18–19

games, 18–19
Genghis Khan, 14–15
"Die Glocke" (weapon), 13

Harald the Ruthless, 10–12
Harriman, W. Averell, 24–25
human nature, 31

Magruder, John B., 22–23
Mongol Empire, 14–15

navies, 16–17
Nazis, 13
North Vietnam, 26–28
nuclear weapons, 29

Ojibwe tribe, 18–19
Ottoman Empire, 16–17

Persian Cat War, 6–7
prisoners of war, 20–21

Roman Empire, 16–17

ships, 16–17
Sigurdsson, Harald, 10–12
South Vietnam, 26, 27
spying, 5, 15, 20–21, 24–25
stealth, 5, 10–12, 14–15, 20–21, 24–25, 26–28

transportation networks, 15, 16–17, 26–28
tunnels, 26–28

Van Lew, Elizabeth, 20–21
Vietcong, 26–28

Vikings, 10–12

war, 4, 30, 31
war technology
bombs, 29
bugs, 24–25
drones, 5
land ships, 16–17
mysteries, 13
war tricks
described, 4, 14–15, 30
personalities and examples, 6–28
weapons collection tricks, 9, 18–19
World War II, 13, 29

Yongqiu, China, 8–9
Yorktown, Virginia, 22–23

Zhang Xun, 8–9